The Coming Civil War

A prophetic view of the coming war within the Church

The Coming Civil War

© Copyright 2009, Daryl C.J. Allen

ISBN 978-0-578-01383-1

Lulu Enterprises, Inc.
860 Aviation Parkway, Suite 300
Morrisville, NC 27560
www.lulu.com

*All scriptures are quoted from various versions
of the Holy Bible. I intentionally put satan's
name in small letters because I chose not to
exalt him in any way even to the extent of being
grammatically incorrect.*

Prepare The Way Ministries
revdcja@yahoo.com

"We have met the enemy, and they are ours"
Commodore Oliver Hazard Perry
August 23, 1785 – August 23, 1819

Table of Contents

The Coming Civil War

A prophetic view of the coming war within the Church

Chapter One
Change is Coming

"There's a war coming to the body of Christ." You might say, duh! We've been in a war. Yes, you're right. We've been a war against the powers of darkness since the beginning of time. But I submit to you we're about to experience a war we've never seen before-a war that will rise within the ranks of the army of the Lord Jesus Christ. This war will be fought believer against believer. It sounds like a major spiritual paradox, but it is very real, and it's coming.

There will be men and women of God who will rise up against one another in a manner that has never been seen or heard of in our modern time. This war will come because of one simple reason-change.

Change has always been the key element to wars within the church. When God brings change to His people by His Spirit it causes a major disruption in our lives and ministries. Many people welcome change because it releases a fresh new perspective and births an excitement in the hearts of those who live continuously in a spirit of expectation to see what's next in their walk with the Almighty. Some abhor change because it takes many out of there places of comfort and daily regiments and rituals. And it's because of these convictions between believers that change has caused many confrontations to take place in the body of Christ. So whether you're open to change or one who resists it, it is of no consequence because, "change is still coming."

*The word change is defined as, **A variation or alteration in form, state, quality, or essence; or a passing from one state or form to another; as a change of countenance; a change of habits or principles.***

1

The Coming Civil War

The change that is coming will be so extreme only those who have received the revelation from God-the Holy Spirit of what's about to happen and have yielded to His preparation will be ready for the indescribable metamorphosis that's coming to the body of Christ. Those who will resist this change will be those who will be the opponents of this major transformation that's coming to the Church and ultimately be at war against the King of heaven.

This change that's coming will disrupt the established status quo of the church and its spiritual condition. This move of God is going to so shake the powers that be and it will destroy anything that doesn't line up with the plans of God.

A vision

During a time of praise and worship in one of our Sunday services, the Lord gave me a vision. In the vision I saw the hand of God reach down into some dry ground and pull out a man. The man whom He pulled out of the ground was alive but had the appearance of being lifeless. As I looked at the man in the hand of God, I noticed he was still covered with dirt and debris from the condition he was brought out from.

All of a sudden, without warning, the hand of God began to violently shake the man, causing the dirt and debris on the man to fly off of him without any opposition.

There's a shaking taking place in the church of Jesus Christ. This shaking is designed to deliver us from the things that are still attached to us from the world and the influence of the enemy.

2

This shaking is going to remove things many of us are still struggling with that have crippled us in various aspect of our lives and walk with God. This is necessary if we are going to be completely free from all that God has delivered us from.

This shaking is also designed to prepare us for the full measure of God's glory He has ordained for us to come into. This glory will release the full measure of the character and nature of Jesus Christ in the lives of His people who have yielded to His will. And although the shaking was violent it was God doing the shaking. Many will misinterpret the violent shaking as the enemy attacking. But this is because of the lack of sensitivity to the movements of the Holy Spirit. When Christ was asked by the pharisees and sadducees (those who were resistant to change) to give them a sign from heaven he had this to say:

> **He answered and said unto them, When it is evening, ye say, It will be fair weather: for the sky is red. And in the morning, It will be foul weather today: for the sky is red and lowering. O ye hypocrites, ye can discern the face of the sky; but can ye not discern the signs of the times?**
> **Matthew 16:2,3**

*As I shared this vision to the congregation, the Lord immediately spoke to me, **"tell My people, the more they resist My shaking, the more violent the shaking will become."** God is determined to set us free in order for His will to be done in the earth.*

The Coming Civil War

The methods in which the Lord uses may be totally confusing to us, but if we can first, understand that it's God doing the shaking, and second, the motive for the shaking, we can then become like the man in the hand of God and just yield. And if the reason isn't revealed, the Lord will assure us that it is by His hand the change is taking place.

And this word, Yet once more, signifieth the removing of those things that are shaken, as of things that are made, that those things which cannot be shaken may remain
Hebrews 12:27

I want to give you some other definitions of change and expound on each of them prophetically that we may understand what I sense God is, not only doing, but going to do in the days to come. As you read these definitions remember, they speak only to those of us who are open to change. As you read this book you may conclude that change is challenging to you. But I pray that as you read on the Spirit of the Lord will give you a new heart that's open for change.

To pass from one state to another

This definition speaks of one passing from one state of being to another state of being. There are people throughout the body of Christ who have had the next season of God revealed to them by the Holy Spirit. And the Holy Spirit does this because He desires our participation in what He's destined to perform.

4

Surely the Lord GOD will do nothing, but he revealeth his secret unto his servants the prophets
Amos 3:7

This is so important to understand. When God reveals things to us it is because He's calling us to be a part of His purposes and plans for mankind and to take on His mindset to see His will done. And because we have seen what the next move of God entails, we realize in order for us to flow in union with the Lord, a change within each of us is required.

The Lord is currently taking His people through a process. This process is designed to kill everything within us that darkens the glory of God in the lives of His people.

Ye are the light of the world. A city that is set on a hill cannot be hid. Neither do men light a candle, and put it under a bushel, but on a candlestick; and it giveth light unto all that are in the house. Let your light so shine before men, that they may see your good works, and glorify your Father which is in heaven
Matthew 5:14-16

As you perform a study on the lampstand which is in the most holy place of the tabernacle, where there is no light but that which comes from the lampstand, if any one of the seven lamps are not burning, then the light within the holy place is darkened, thus affecting the priest's vision and making his ability to fulfill his purpose more difficult.

5

The Coming Civil War

It is vital that we allow the Spirit of God to both will and to do of His good pleasure in each of our lives that the light of His presence may shine without hindrance from those of us who call ourselves the redeemed. It's only through the revelation of God's presence in the lives of His people that those who dwells in darkness can see the light of Christ's love and power, and ultimately be drawn into the kingdom of God.

We haven't just come to an end of one year and are entering into a new year, but we're coming to the end of the season of the Lord's preparation and are about to enter into a season of the glory of God the world has never seen before. I would be so bold to say that even the days when our Lord Himself walked the earth will pale in comparison to the glory that's about to be revealed in the lives of God's people who have given themselves completely to the will of God.

Verily, verily, I say unto you, He that believeth on me, the works that I do shall he do also; and greater works than these shall he do; because I go unto my Father
John 14:12

To change the heart or life

When people speak of a change of heart they immediately think of or reach toward the physical organ. But this isn't the heart the bible speaks of. When the bible speaks of a change of heart it speaks of a change in one's thinking and feelings. Some of the translations of the word heart speaks of the intellect, the emotions, and the volition or will.

6

In other words we're looking at a soulish change that's going to take place in the lives of God's people. This change will be so extreme that many will be completely transformed because their minds have been completely renewed and they will walk and function from a spiritual paradigm rather than an earthly one. This will bring about a people that will be completely consecrated unto to the Lord; A people that will no longer walk in a state of compromise or worldly lust or corruption, but will declare even as Lord Jesus did, "Repent! For the kingdom of heaven is at hand."

Repent (change your mind for the better, heartily amend your ways, with abhorrence of your past sins), for the kingdom of heaven is at hand
Matthew 4:17
The Amplified Version

As a result of this transformation in the minds of God's people, we will begin to see a greater demonstration of the power of God in the earth. We will begin to truly see what the kingdom of God is supposed to be like in the lives of the Lord's people. We will see a people walking in divine life, health, strength, and power. There will be no more sickness, diseases, or afflictions in the lives of God's people who have submitted to the change. We will see God's people walking in the ways and thoughts of the Lord and doing His perfect will, taking nothing from or adding nothing to His perfect plan. We will see such a change in the minds of the people there will be a visible distinction between the people of God and the lost.

7

To shift

  One the day of Pentecost the 120 in the upper room were praying and waiting for the promise of the Father which Lord Jesus had told them would come. They had no idea what the day would be, nor the hour when the promise of God would manifest. But they also had no idea that the power that was about to be released into their lives would be of such a degree that their lives would be change forever.

  A major shift is about to manifest in the body of Christ. What was once considered normal will be instantly done away with. This paradigm shift will literally snatch the body of Christ into a new dimension the body of Christ has never experienced before. To adjust to this sudden change is going to require God's people to give themselves over to prayer, unity, peace, and submission to the will and presence of the Holy Spirit. This shift also requires the people of God to be obedient to strategic positioning. The disciples received instructions from God to go position themselves in Jerusalem and remain there until the Holy Spirit is released into the earth. Position is vital for change to occur. God will speak to us to be in a specific position to receive the promise that will produce change in our lives and the lives of others. To be out of position creates a breach in the plans of God and derails the move of His Spirit. A day of sudden change is about to overtake us and we must be prepare to shift with God.

Behold, I will do a new thing; now it shall
spring forth; shall ye not know it?
Isaiah 43:19a

A succession of one thing in the place of another

Throughout the word of God we see a changing of authority in the children of Israel. Joshua succeeded Moses. Samuel succeeded Eli. David succeeded Saul. Solomon succeeded David. And Elisha succeeded Elijah. In this next move of God's Spirit we will see a succession of authority throughout the Church. There are many men and women whom God has taken through years of preparation for this season that's about to overtake us. These people will walk in the character and nature of God in a way never before seen. They shall walk in an unprecedented power and authority that will literally catapult the Church from a mentality of a religious, divided, weak entity to a powerful and glorious force walking in the mind of Christ and a resolve to establish the kingdom of God in the earth. Through this sudden succession we see God, through His new kingdom leadership, bring forth a massive influx of souls into the kingdom of God.

Some of the new leadership will be those whom God has set aside in a long season of obscurity and preparation. But there will be some who are already in position who have receive the revelation of change and they have given themselves over to the work of God and they have allow the Holy Spirit to work in them both to will and do of His good pleasure. And through their willingness to humble themselves and allow God to birth change within them, they will be a part of the season of succession in the body of Christ.

Just as there will be those in leadership who will acknowledge this change in spiritual leadership, there will be those who will intensely oppose this season of change.

The Coming Civil War

This opposition was evident in the time of Saul and how he used all his power and resources to destroy David, who was symbolic of the new move of God coming in the form of new leadership, coming into contact with His people and doing away with the carnal, controlling, rebellious, idolatrous leadership and bringing them back to obedience, worship, and submission to the laws and commands of God.

But Saul, who is symbolic of the carnal, controlling, religious, rebellious, idolatrous leadership will intensely come against the new leadership God is replacing them with because of the threat of destruction to the kingdom which they were building unto themselves and their unwillingness to submit to the change and commands of God.

We see this evident not only in the time of Saul and David, but in the time of our Lord in His war against the sanhedrin. Even though they saw the wonderful works of God manifesting through Lord Jesus, they refuse to submit to the new leadership of God in demonstration in the earth. Just as we've read of the power and demonstration of Lord Jesus, we'll see that same power and authority demonstrated in the lives and ministries of the new leadership. As the sandhedrin of His day came against Him, we'll see the modern day sanhedrin come against the new leadership as well.

Remember the word that I said unto you, The servant is not greater than his lord. If they have persecuted me, they will also persecute you; if they have kept my saying, they will keep yours also
John 15:20

10

Not only did the pharisees and sadducees resist Lord Jesus, they came against everyone who embraced the new move of God taking place in the land. There will be many of God's people who will embrace the move of God, that will experience intense persecution by the sanhedrin of our day.

We will see three types of people in the Church that will arise in the next move of God. We will see people who will openly embrace the move of God but will suffer great persecution. We will see people who embrace the move of God, but will not embrace it openly to avoid persecution by those opposed to it. These people will be like a modern day Nicademus who will come to Jesus by night to experience His love, power, and glory. They will desire the new thing but they will be in a spiritual and emotional quandary, being afraid to divorce themselves from that which they know is obsolete and yet they will remain because of displaced loyalty. But there will be some who will openly resist the change and stand by their sandhedrin leadership. They will not just resist and fight the new move of God, but they will ultimately find themselves fighting God (Acts 5:34-39).

This war will go on until the old is completely done away with as the new becomes more and more power in the earth through the increased presence, power, and authority of the Almighty.

Now there was long war between the house of Saul and the house of David: but David waxed stronger and stronger, and the house of Saul waxed weaker and weaker
II Samuel 3:1
11

A revolution

The word revolution is defined as, **"a course or motion which brings every point of the surface back to the place at which it began to move."**

> **For the creature was made subject to vanity, not willingly, but by reason of him who hath subjected the same in hope, Because the creature itself also shall be delivered from the bondage of corruption into the glorious liberty of the children of God. For we know that the whole creation groaneth and travaileth in pain together until now. And not only they, but ourselves also, which have the firstfruits of the Spirit, even we ourselves groan within ourselves, waiting for the adoption, to wit, the redemption of our body**
> **Romans 8:20-23**

We are about to witness the greatest restorational move of God in the history of the world and of mankind. We will see men and women of God restored to oneness, not only with the Father, but also with all of creation. We see this evident in Adam and in Lord Jesus' life.

Before Adam fell he was in union with the Father and with creation. All of creation was subject to him. After the fall, Christ came in the fullness of time and revealed to us through His life what a man created in the image of God was supposed to look and function like.

And as Lord Jesus walked in the full image, power, and authority of the Father (Hebrews 1:1-3), as He demonstrated the kingdom of God and His rule over all of creation, we will walk in the full image, power, and authority of the Son of God.

For whom he did foreknow, he also did predestinate to be conformed to the image of his Son, that he might be the firstborn among many brethren
Romans 8:29

We will see a company of saints of God, walking in the fullness of the Spirit, demonstrating the love and nature of God. By this manifestation of the presence of God in the lives of His people we will see an unprecedented change in society. We'll see a change in the market place. We'll see a change in the family structure. We'll see a change in the governmental structure. We'll see a change in the educational system. Millions of young people will turn to God. Reconciliation will take place among families that have been separated for years. Crime will literally become almost non-existent. Abuse will cease. Poverty will disappear. Drug addiction, dealing, and abuse will dissipate. Abortion will cease. The children of light will finally become wiser the children of the world. The fear of the lord will be restored in the lives of His people. The Church of the Lord Jesus Christ will be unified and be more powerful than she has ever been. All forms of isms and schisms will be done away with and true praise and worship to the true and living God will be restored back to the land.

13

The Coming Civil War

In the coming chapters we'll take a deeper look at what the coming war within the Church will be like. I pray that as you read this book, the Holy Spirit will speak to you like never before. I pray as you allow the Spirit of the Lord to have His way, He will reveal to you where you may be resisting Him and allow Him to do away with that area of hardness and come into a place of complete submission to His will for your life that you may not find yourself fighting against Him in the days to come.

This next move of God will not only have unprecedented glory but with it will come unprecedented opposition and we must be so united with the Lord we will be prepared for the battles that lay ahead.

This will truly be a spiritual battle of the ages. It will be time many relationships will be severed but new relationships will be forged.

This will not just be a battle of the spirit, but it will be a battle of the flesh. We'll be challenged like never before mentally and emotionally and it will take the power of God to see us through every challenge we encounter.

We'll see the judgment of God manifest in the land. There will be times that we'll cry out to God for His mercy and He will hear our prayers. But there will be times we'll cry out to God for His mercy and He will tell us to get out of the way.

Let us go deeper now and see what God is saying and pray for God's will to be done in our lives and that He will prepare us for what's coming.

Chapter 2
The Coming Glory

But as truly as I live, all the earth shall be filled with the glory of the LORD
Numbers 14:21

Over the past 5 or 10 years the Lord has given me several dreams relating to the next great outpouring of the Holy Spirit in the Land. In this chapter I will share one of those dreams with you and the revelation I've received from God. Through these interpretations I pray we will receive deeper insight as to, not only what God is currently doing, and what He's about to do, but what we need to do to prepare for the coming glory of God.

There were wells throughout the land

Not long ago, the Lord gave me a dream. In that dream, it was a quiet beautiful day, the sky was blue, and the clouds were a pure white. The land was full of rolling hills and rich green grass. And as far as the eye could see there were wells. These wells were made of white cobble-like stones and they all were exactly the same size, shape, and color.

Suddenly, the earth began to quake. Then, I was taken underground, beneath the wells. And as the ground shook, I could see water beginning to rise beneath each one of the wells. The water was rising slowly but powerfully.

Then, I was taken back to the surface to the original scene, but this time the land was quaking because of the rising water that was about to burst forth.

Then all of a sudden, the water came forth.

The Coming Civil War

But it didn't come forth like a mighty force as I thought it would in relation to the way the earth was quaking. But it just gradually flowed out from the wells onto the ground. The interesting thing about this water was that I was clear, thick and appeared to be alive. And as it began to cover the ground it didn't soak into the ground as normal water naturally would. But it just began to cover the ground and spread throughout the land. Then the dream ended.

The above scripture speaks of God's glory covering the earth as the water cover the sea and this dream will confirm this as we delve deeper into it to see more of what God has to say to us.

The day of peace and beauty is really a day of change. This is a day which speaks of peace but it is a day in which great change is taking place. It is a day in which from a natural perspective, the beauty, the peace and quiet have caused many, including many in the body of Christ, to be lulled into a false sense of peace and security. It is a day in which on the surface it appears peaceful but under the surface a shaking and a great change is taking place. Great shifts under the earth's crust are taking place. And as this is taking place in the natural, there is an event taking place behind the scenes in the Spirit realm and in the souls of many men and women in the body of Christ

**For when they shall say, Peace and safety;
then sudden destruction cometh upon them, as
travail upon a woman with child; and they
shall not escape
I Thessalonians 5:3**

*This day of peace and solitude is also known as **"the day of the Lord."** This is the day in which God will perform all that the prophets have prophesied from the days of Noah until the time of the Apostle John. This is the day in which the proud and lofty shall be brought low and the humble shall be exalted in the glory of the Lord.*

> **For the day of the LORD of hosts shall be**
> **upon every one that is proud and lofty, and**
> **upon every one that is lifted up; and he shall**
> **be brought low**
> **Isaiah 2:12**

This is a time when the people of God must be in tuned with the movement and workings of the Holy Spirit to have an understanding of the times and seasons to know what the body of Christ must be doing. There is a changing of the seasons taking place and if the people of God are not prepared we may find ourselves missing the experience of walking in the glory of our God and fulfilling our destiny.

> **And of the children of Issachar, which were**
> **men that had understanding of the times, to**
> **know what Israel ought to do**
> **I Chronicles 12:32**

This is a time in which the watch and the prophetic are crucial to the Church. Those of us called to be watchman and prophets are in a time which praying and hearing from God must be relayed with accuracy and in God's timing.

**I will stand upon my watch, and set me upon
the tower, and will watch to see what he will
say unto me, and what I shall answer when I
am reproved
Habakkuk 2:1**

**Surely the Lord GOD will do nothing, but he
revealeth his secret unto his servants the
prophets
Amos 3:7**

*The prophets and the intercessors are the eyes, ears,
and voice of God in the Church. These ministries are vital for
accurate communication to flow from heaven to earth. The
prophets and intercessors are the vehicles which God uses to
transmit His will and intentions to the body of Christ and the
men and women He has prepared and strategically positioned
throughout the land (the wells) to release His will (the glory)
into the land thereby causing the kingdom of God to be
released and expand thus covering the earth as the waters
cover the sea.*

*The body of Christ must have their senses quicken to
recognize the operation of the Lord. We as the people of God
must transcend the world's perspective and come into our
inheritance of seeing in the Spirit the things which God has
prepared for them that love Him (I Corinthians 2:9,10).*

**For yourselves know perfectly that the day of
the Lord so cometh as a thief in the night
I Thessalonians 5:2**

This is a day that will seem to the carnal minded person a day of solitude and comfort but it is a day in which God has commanded His glory to be released in the earth.

And the glory of the LORD shall be revealed, and all flesh shall see it together: for the mouth of the LORD hath spoken it
Isaiah 40:5

This is a day of shaking. And this great shaking has begun in the Church. This is necessary because the Church has taken the things of the world and the lies from the enemy and incorporated them into the purpose and plan of God. For the glory of God to be seen in His people, He must first cleanse us. He must first prune us. He must first purify us. And He must first remove everything that life, religion, generations, and satan has infected His bride with so she can become who she was created to be. And when that which can be shaken has been shaken off, that which cannot be shaken will manifest, be seen, and remain (Hebrews 12:25-28).

The shaking is just that, a shaking. It is a divine disruption, dislocation, and disorientation by the Lord of that which has been established by religion, tradition, and satan. The shaking is designed by God to disrupt the normal flow and operation of immorality, corruption, and apostasy in the earth. All things must be restored according to the redemptive plan of God. In this next move of God we will see the redemptive order of God come to full fruition in the earth. We will see the glory of God in the earth on a scale never before seen since the day that our Lord walked the earth in the flesh.

19

The shaking on the surface is but a secondary response to that which is taking place under the earth. The enormous amount of water pressure built up beneath the earth over a long period of time causes the water to be pushed upward to the surface. This causes the shaking on the surface.

God is shaking the earth by His Spirit. It is a divine shaking that is affecting not just the body of Christ but all of creation. This is a shaking that's a result of the Spirit of God pushing His way through the earth. He's moving His way through the carnality and immorality of man's ways, will, and desires, pressing His way and forcing Himself to the forefront to take His rightful place, establishing His kingdom, power, and glory in the earth and in the lives of His people.

**Thy kingdom come. Thy will be done in earth,
as it is in heaven
Matthew 6:10**

The Spirit of God is shaking every realm of society. He's shaking the governments. He's shaking the scientific community. He's shaking the educational community. He's shaking the justice system. He's shaking the family structure. He's shaking the medical community. He's shaking the market place. And He's shaking all realms of faith, including Christianity itself.

**I will shake the heavens, and the earth...And I
will shake all nations...and I will fill this
house with glory, saith the LORD of hosts
Haggai 2:6,7**

20

We're seeing a shaking in the form of wars, in both local governments and between nations. We're seeing a shaking in communities. We're seeing shaking families. And we are seeing a shaking taking place in the very house of God. This is very necessary for God to rid us of all that religion, tradition, satan, and the flesh has incorporated into the body of Christ which has been accepted as divine.

God is a jealous God. He is a God that will not allow anything or anyone to take His place of prominence in the lives of His people. And unfortunately this has taken place throughout the body of Christ.

Many of God's people have lost focus, replacing the vision of the kingdom with seeking prosperity, notoriety, materialism, titles, position and power. We've made the word of God of none effect because of the lust of the flesh, the lust of the eyes and the pride of life; the very thing that caused Adam to loose his position in the beginning. And as a result the Church has become like the valley of dry bones, we've become parched, divided, and lifeless (Ezekiel 37:1,2). But God is shaking us and taking His rightful place and restoring the order of God back into the hearts of His people.

For in my jealousy and in the fire of my wrath
have I spoken, Surely in that day there shall be
a great shaking in the land of Israel
Ezekiel 38:19

The wells speak of the people of God. These are the corporate wells of the kingdom of God, built up strong, dug deep in character, and whose foundation is sure.

21

The Coming Civil War

These are those who have been built up as the lively stones by the inner workings of the Holy Spirit to walk the earth in the image of Jesus Who is our pattern Son.

> **For whom he did foreknow, he also did predestinate to be conformed to the image of his Son, that he might be the firstborn among many brethren**
> **Romans 8:29**

> **Ye also, as lively stones, are built up a spiritual house, an holy priesthood, to offer up spiritual sacrifices, acceptable to God by Jesus Christ**
> **I Peter 2:5**

The wells were all over the land, as far as the eye could see. These are the people of God who have been strategically positioned throughout the land according to the will of God to be the conduits for the release of the glory of God in every area of society.

> **Behold, God is my salvation; I will trust, and not be afraid: for the LORD JEHOVAH is my strength and my song; he also is become my salvation. Therefore with joy shall ye draw water out of the wells of salvation**
> **Isaiah 12:2,3**

These are men and women, chosen by God before the foundation of the world to be the carriers of His glory.

These are they which have been sanctified from the world and set apart to be instruments of the Almighty for this last great move of His Spirit.

As the well is dug deep to tap into the river that lies beneath the earth, so to has the Lord done a deep work in the hearts of His chosen. They have been taken through a severe process to cleanse and purify them for the great work they've been called to perform. They have been shaped and molded, pruned, and purged to be the vessels fit for the master's use. They are being built from the same pattern, which is Christ Jesus to walk in and demonstrate the character of our God.

These are they which will walk in the image and likeness of Lord Jesus Christ, who will shake the foundation of the earth by the power and demonstration of the Spirit and will release out of their innermost being rivers of living water, the very glory of God into the earth.

In the last day, that great day of the feast, Jesus stood and cried, saying, If any man thirst, let him come unto me, and drink. He that believeth on me, as the Scripture hath said, out of his belly shall flow rivers of living water.
John 7:37,38

We're about to see the manifestation of the very presence and glory of God invading nations. Chosen men and women around the world will walk in the glory of God in a manner never before seen in the history of Christendom. It will even exceed the day when Lord Jesus walked the earth.

23

**Verily, verily, I say unto you, He that believeth
on me, the works that I do shall he do also;
and greater works than these shall he do;
because I go unto my Father
John 14:12**

The water overflowed and began to cover the earth.
This is the living water. That life giving water which the Lord
prophesied would spring forth from the innermost being of
His chosen vessels. This is the manifested presence of God-
the Holy Spirit covering the earth as He promised.

**For the earth shall be filled with the
knowledge of the glory of the LORD, as the
waters cover the sea
Habakkuk 2:14**

As we look at the dream we can see that each well was
overflowing with living water. What this dream doesn't
literally reveal is that as the water continues the flow out of
the wells, eventually we will see the water from one well
flowing out and connecting with the water that's flowing from
another well. And as this continues we'll see the water cover
the earth as our Lord prophecied. We will see the people of
the land covered and saturated with the outpouring of the
Holy Spirit as prophesied by the prophet Joel.

**And it shall come to pass afterward, that I will
pour out my spirit upon all flesh
Joel 2:28a**

24

The grass is the people of the earth. They are the people of the land that will experience the overwhelming outpouring of the Holy Spirit that shall spring forth from with the men and women of God that shall release the glory of God from within their innermost beings. And all flesh shall see and experience the presence and glory of Almighty God.

And the glory of the LORD shall be revealed, and all flesh shall see it together: for the mouth of the LORD hath spoken it. The voice said, Cry. And he said, What shall I cry? All flesh is grass, and all the goodliness thereof is as the flower of the field
Isaiah 40:5,6

God is bringing His people into agreement with His plan, not just for ourselves, but for all of mankind. He's positioning His people throughout the earth, doing a deep work in us to tap into the life-giving presence of the Holy Spirit that's going to come forth like rivers to overflow the banks of all humanity, saturating the hearts of all that are open to receive His love, grace, mercy, healing, deliverance, and salvation.

Behold, God is my salvation; I will trust, and not be afraid: for the LORD JEHOVAH is my strength and my song; he also is become my salvation. Therefore with joy shall ye draw water out of the wells of salvation
Isaiah 12:2,3

In the last day, that great day of the feast, Jesus stood and cried, saying, If any man thirst, let him come unto me, and drink. He that believeth on me, as the Scripture hath said, out of his belly shall flow rivers of living water.
John 7:37,38

The coming glory is already in the earth. It is the treasure hidden in the earthen vessels of God.

But we have this treasure in earthen vessels, that the excellency of the power may be of God, and not of us
II Corinthians 4:7

God is digging deep in the souls of His people for that exceeding and eternal weight of glory to break forth for all flesh shall see His fullness in the lives of His people. This is the only way those that dwell in darkness can see the Lord. The glory of God must shine to lead a dying world to Christ.

Arise, shine; for thy light is come, and the glory of the LORD is risen upon thee. For, behold, the darkness shall cover the earth, and gross darkness the people: but the LORD shall arise upon thee, and his glory shall be seen upon thee. And the Gentiles shall come to thy light, and kings to the brightness of thy rising
Isaiah 60:1-3

Chapter 3
The Demonstration of the Spirit

*AS FOR myself, brethren, when I came to you,
I did not come proclaiming to you the
testimony and evidence or mystery and secret
of God [concerning what He has done through
Christ for the salvation of men] in lofty words
of eloquence or human philosophy and
wisdom; For I resolved to know nothing (to be
acquainted with nothing, to make a display of
the knowledge of nothing, and to be conscious
of nothing) among you except Jesus Christ
and Him crucified. And I was in (passed into a
state of) weakness and fear (dread) and great
trembling [after I had come] among you. And
my language and my message were not set
forth in persuasive (enticing and plausible)
words of wisdom, but they were in
demonstration of the [Holy] Spirit and power
[a proof by the Spirit and power of God,
operating on me and stirring in the minds of
my hearers the most holy emotions and thus
persuading them], So that your faith might not
rest in the wisdom of men (human
philosophy), but in the power of God.*
I Corinthians 2:1-5
The Amplified Version

*The coming move of the Holy Spirit will be a move of
God like nothing He has ever done in the history of mankind.
This will be the season of the demonstration of God.*

27

The Coming Civil War

We see Paul, in the above scripture, sharing with the saints at Corinth, a revelation of the utter futility of man's wisdom and ability to properly articulate the things of the Spirit concerning Lord Jesus. He lets them know there is nothing on this earthly plain, with all of man's knowledge and philosophical discourse that can with accuracy, power, and life-changing articulation that can truly impart a clear and precise account of the goodness and glory of God and the sacrifice of our blessed Savior. This has been the epicenter of the Church's problem and impotency of the body of Christ for many hundreds of years.

Throughout history we see men and women who proclaim to be the servants of the Almighty move in religious dogma and the traditions of men and in every dispensation of the Church without fail shutting down the move of God because of their carnal reasoning and the enemy's influence. And anyone that came forth with new fresh revelation from the throne of God were judged as heretics and fanatics and should be ignored, commanded to renounce their doctrine, excommunicated from the Church, or put to death.

Paul lets the people know that the eloquence of words and the poetic presentation of man's discourse may be beautiful but lacks the power that is necessary to set the captives free and exalt the name of the Lord Jesus Christ. This form of dissertation, although beautiful and eloquent, is also the evidence of man's arrogance, fleshly ways and an indication of man placing himself at the forefront rather than in the background. This is one of many reasons why we as the people of God have become in many circles in society around the world the laughing stock of the human race.

But as the man of God shares with us the problem with the Church he also gives us the solution. But this solution is also the enemy of the problem. The solution is the enemy of the problem because it says nothing of exalting man but exalting God. When this type of mentality invades the religious and the traditional a war breaks out in a place where there's supposed to be unity, peace, joy, and love.

Lord Jesus shares with us if there's going to be peace, joy, and love in the lives of His people throughout the earth it's going to come through war.

> **Think not that I am come to send peace on earth: I came not to send peace, but a sword. For I am come to set a man at variance against his father, and the daughter against her mother, and the daughter-in-law against her mother-in-law. And a man's foes shall be they of his own household**
> **Matthew 10:34-36**

Both Lord Jesus and Paul were speaking on the demonstration of the Spirit. Lord Jesus and Paul moved in the manifestation and demonstration of the Holy Spirit which brought about great variance and opposition throughout the land. And just as this took place in the days when Lord Jesus and Paul walked the earth, it shall take place again with those whom God will use in this next move of His Spirit.

The word demonstration is defined as, **"Indubitable evidence of the senses or of reason; evidence which satisfies the mind of the certainty of a fact or proposition."**

29

The Coming Move of God

The world has been furiously debating over what is the true faith and religion for thousands of years. This conflict has brought about more wars, destruction, and even death than any political or governmental dispute a thousand times over. Millions of men and women throughout the history of mankind have willingly given their lives for the cause of their faith. Some have given up worldly possessions and have even sacrificed their families all for their faith. But the one element that all of the thousands of various faiths in the world cannot do is call on their god to manifest and demonstrate to the world their presence and power, except Christianity.

And Elijah came unto all the people, and said, How long halt ye between two opinions? if the LORD be God, follow him: but if Baal, then follow him. And the people answered him not a word. Then said Elijah unto the people, I, even I only, remain a prophet of the LORD; but Baal's prophets are four hundred and fifty men. Let them therefore give us two bullocks; and let them choose one bullock for themselves, and cut it in pieces, and lay it on wood, and put no fire under: and I will dress the other bullock, and lay it on wood, and put no fire under: And call ye on the name of your gods, and I will call on the name of the LORD: and the God that answereth by fire, let him be God. And all the people answered and said, It is well spoken...

30

And they took the bullock which was given them, and they dressed it, and called on the name of Baal from morning even until noon, saying, O Baal, hear us. But there was no voice, nor any that answered. And they leaped upon the altar which was made...And it came to pass, when midday was past, and they prophesied until the time of the offering of the evening sacrifice, that there was neither voice, nor any to answer, nor any that regarded.... And it came to pass at the time of the offering of the evening sacrifice, that Elijah the prophet came near, and said, LORD God of Abraham, Isaac, and of Israel, let it be known this day that thou art God in Israel, and that I am thy servant, and that I have done all these things at thy word. Hear me, O LORD, hear me, that this people may know that thou art the LORD God, and that thou hast turned their heart back again. Then the fire of the LORD fell, and consumed the burnt sacrifice, and the wood, and the stones, and the dust, and licked up the water that was in the trench. And when all the people saw it, they fell on their faces: and they said, The LORD, he is the God; the LORD, he is the God.
I Kings 18:21-24,26,29,36-39

In Hebrew demonstration means, **"To show forth, to view, or to exhibit."**

31

The Coming Civil War

This is why servants of God such as Benny Hinn, Rinhard Bonke, Oral and Richard Roberts, Rodney Howard-Browne, and Marilyn Hickey have such a massive success rate in converting souls. It is because they submit to and allow the manifestation and demonstration of the presence and power of God. This is the one element in our faith that answers any questions of what faith is really the true faith and puts all critiques and religious opponents to shame and silence, the manifestation and demonstration of the Spirit.

And I, brethren, when I came to you, came not with excellency of speech or of wisdom, declaring unto you the testimony of God. For I determined not to know any thing among you, save Jesus Christ, and him crucified. And I was with you in weakness, and in fear, and in much trembling. And my speech and my preaching was not with enticing words of man's wisdom, but in demonstration of the Spirit and of power: That your faith should not stand in the wisdom of men, but in the power of God
I Corinthians 2:1-5

But with this great privilege comes great opposition. Opposition outside the Church from other faiths because millions of muslims, buddhist, cultics, occultics, and family members are turning their backs on old lifestyles and false religious practices to embrace all that Christ has for them.

But inside the Church, the opposition comes from men and women in leadership who refuse to change and remain faithful to false and or distorted doctrine and the traditions of men. This hostile opposition will intensify because of the rapid decline of membership and people they control and influence who are coming into the knowledge of the Truth and are breaking free from the bondages that blinded them and once held them captive. Because many are afraid and threatened that their established way of doing things will cease because of the power of God turning the hearts and minds of the lost from darkness, religion, and bondage to liberty, joy, peace, and destiny.

**The Spirit of the Lord is upon me, because he hath anointed me to preach the gospel to the poor; he hath sent me to heal the brokenhearted, to preach deliverance to the captives, and recovering of sight to the blind, to set at liberty them that are bruised, To preach the acceptable year of the Lord
Luke 4:18,19**

The manifestation and demonstration of the Holy Spirit is the one event that will change the fabric and course of society. Every level of the social structure of the civilized world will be transformed. From the local daycare center to the governmental structure, all of mankind will be deeply and eternally impacted by the Spirit of the living God. In this next manifestation of the Holy Spirit we will see cities changed by the manifestation and demonstration of the power of God.

> **Then Philip went down to the city of Samaria,**
> **and preached Christ unto them. And the**
> **people with one accord gave heed unto those**
> **things which Philip spake, hearing and seeing**
> **the miracles which he did. For unclean spirits,**
> **crying with loud voice, came out of many that**
> **were possessed with them: and many taken**
> **with palsies, and that were lame, were healed.**
> **And there was great joy in that city**
> **Acts 8:5-8**

Prior to Philip's arrival at Samaria, Samaria was a city deeply seduced, controlled, and influenced by fear, witchcraft, and idolatry.

> **But there was a certain man, called Simon,**
> **which beforetime in the same city used**
> **sorcery, and bewitched the people of Samaria,**
> **giving out that himself was some great one: To**
> **whom they all gave heed, from the least to the**
> **greatest, saying, This man is the great power**
> **of God. And to him they had regard, because**
> **that of long time he had bewitched them with**
> **sorceries**
> **Acts 8:9-11**

People in positions of leadership around the world are being seduced and influenced by principalities and powers that are implementing the purpose and plans of the kingdom of darkness to gain a strategic foothold in different regions.

There are eyewitness and documented reports from various sources that governmental leaders in many countries have even submitted to and are being personally advised by witches, warlocks, psychics, and witch doctors on governmental issues. Through this deceptive operation demonic activity has blanketed those nations. But we're coming to the day when we'll see the glory of God break forth and bring down every principality, power, and rulers of darkness that have been killing, stealing and destroying regions for hundreds of years. And in a single day, through the manifestation and demonstration of the Spirit of God, we will see millions of men and women from every corner of the globe give their hearts to the Lord Jesus Christ.

And it shall come to pass in the last days, that the mountain of the LORD's house shall be established in the top of the mountains, and shall be exalted above the hills; and all nations shall flow unto it...And he will lift up an ensign to the nations from far, and will hiss unto them from the end of the earth: and, behold, they shall come with speed swiftly
Isaiah 2:2; Isaiah 5:26

All the ends of the world shall remember and turn unto the LORD: and all the kindreds of the nations shall worship before thee...Yea, all kings shall fall down before him: all nations shall serve him
Psalm 22:27; Psalm 72:11

Millions heal in a day

**And great multitudes came unto him, having
with them those that were lame, blind, dumb,
maimed, and many others, and cast them down
at Jesus' feet; and he healed them: Insomuch
that the multitude wondered, when they saw
the dumb to speak, the maimed to be whole,
the lame to walk, and the blind to see: and they
glorified the God of Israel
Matthew 15:30,31**

*The key element that will bring glory and honor to the
Most High God is when multiplied millions are saved, healed,
and delivered by the power of God. It isn't when we bring the
people to the Church, but when we bring the people to Lord
Jesus. And when we bring them to Lord Jesus we'll see
results. For it is through the demonstration of God's love by
dealing with the issues of the masses that the masses will give
their hearts to the Lord and serve Him exclusively.*

Information vs. Demonstration

*The world is smaller through information. Much of this
information is what the apostle Paul calls "man's wisdom."
This is the heart of man's destruction.*

**There is a way that seemeth right unto a man,
but the end thereof are the ways of death
Proverbs 16:25**

This man's wisdom has brought millions of searching souls into fear and confusion because they just don't know what to believe. They have put their trust in so many people, places and things and have ended up disappointed, betrayed, and let down. People have had information stuffed down their throats and all they've ended up with is confusion. Many have even turned their backs on the Church because we are so divided amongst ourselves we don't know what to believe.

We're divided amongst ourselves because of doctrinal beliefs, which is nothing more than religious information. We are putting out information that contradicts other information that is being put out and all it does is cause division and a lack of trust. We believe that Jesus is Lord. We believe that He's the Chief cornerstone. We believe that He's our foundation. But then we begin to build on that foundation in different way and there is where we confuse the people.

For we are laborers together with God: ye are God's husbandry, ye are God's building. According to the grace of God which is given unto me, as a wise masterbuilder, I have laid the foundation, and another buildeth thereon. But let every man take heed how he buildeth thereupon
I Corinthians 3:9,10

But take heed lest by any means this liberty of yours become a stumblingblock to them that are weak
I Corinthians 8:9

The Coming Civil War

Many forms of information have become the stumbling block for many and has caused them to make decisions that have effected the way they do business, the way they raise their families, the way they deal the world, the way they handle their finances, and even the way we deal with our Lord and Savior. We receive revelation from the Lord to share with the people to edify, exhort, correct, and comfort, but the revelation has been watered down and become information because it has been distorted and tainted by the reasoning of man. We take what God has imparted to us and have added or taken from that which He desires to release to His people. We move in our flesh by our wisdom rather than His Spirit and revelation.

Now before I go any further let me just say this. I'm not opposed to information. There is information out there that's valuable and necessary for progress and development. But when you are part of an organization that is not in agreement with itself, one department is issuing information and another department is issuing information that contradicts the information the other department is issuing, this organization has the potential to destroy lives. And sadly enough, the Church is guilty of this.

And knowing their thoughts, He said to them, Any kingdom that is divided against itself and is being brought to desolation; and laid waste, and no city or house divided against itself will continue to stand
Matthew 12:25
The Amplified Version
38

Millions of people have suffered and died because of wrong information. But I thank God that we are transitioning from information back to revelation and demonstration. God is raising up a people that will no longer add to or take from what He imparts. He is working a work in His chosen people that will bring them into a mindset of submission and extreme obedience to the will and the word of the Father. These chosen vessels are going to walk in the mind of Christ and demonstration the power, glory, and love of the Father.

And I looked, and, lo, a Lamb stood on the mount Zion, and with him a hundred forty and four thousand, having his Father's name written in their foreheads. And I heard a voice from heaven, as the voice of many waters, and as the voice of a great thunder: and I heard the voice of harpers harping with their harps: And they sung as it were a new song before the throne, and before the four beasts, and the elders: and no man could learn that song but the hundred and forty and four thousand, which were redeemed from the earth. These are they which were not defiled with women; for they are virgins. These are they which follow the Lamb whithersoever he goeth. These were redeemed from among men, being the firstfruits unto God and to the Lamb. And in their mouth was found no guile: for they are without fault before the throne of God
Revelation 14:1-5

The Coming Civil War

The enemy has flooded the minds and hearts of mankind with all forms of false information. satan has strategically and successfully released darkness into the earth and have consumed the minds and hearts of people all over the earth through false doctrine, revelation, and caused the people to follow all sorts of false deities and giving themselves over to horrific forms of rituals.

For, behold, the darkness shall cover the earth, and gross darkness the people
Isaiah 60:2a

But if our gospel be hid, it is hid to them that are lost: In whom the god of this world hath blinded the minds of them which believe not, lest the light of the glorious gospel of Christ, who is the image of God, should shine unto them
II Corinthians 4:3,4

But I see the glory of God being released upon the earth through His chosen vessels that will destroy the darkness of satan's influence so the world may know the truth and love of God and receive Lord Jesus Christ as their Savior.

Arise, shine; for thy light is come, and the glory of the LORD is risen upon thee…And the Gentiles shall come to thy light, and kings to the brightness of thy rising
Isaiah 60:1,3

Chapter 4
When the Fire falls

     Of all the kings that sat upon the throne of Israel before and after him, ahab was by far the most wicked of them all. He had absolutely no respect for God or His statutes. The bible says in I Kings 16:31that it was a light thing for him to sin against God. ahab went so far as to marry a women of the zidonians named jezebel who was the daughter of the king ethbaal, who worshipped god called baal.

     Now it was one thing for ahab to marry a woman of the land which was a sin in itself.

> **Neither shalt thou make marriages with them;**
> **thy daughter thou shalt not give unto his son,**
> **nor his daughter shalt thou take unto thy son.**
> **For they will turn away thy son from following**
> **me, that they may serve other gods: so will the**
> **anger of the LORD be kindled against you,**
> **and destroy thee suddenly**
> **Deuteronomy 7:3,4**

But ahab went so far as to forsake God entirely to worship and serve the zidonian god baal.

> **And it came to pass, as if it had been a light**
> **thing for him to walk in the sins of Jeroboam**
> **the son of Nebat, that he took to wife Jezebel**
> **the daughter of Ethbaal king of the Zidonians,**
> **and went and served Baal, and worshiped him**
> **I Kings 16:31**

41

Because of ahab's acts of rebellion, idolatry, and ungodly marriage he lead the entire nation of Israel deeper and deeper into the depths of sin, idolatry, fornication, demonic control and all forms of degradation.

Unfortunately, this is the issue today in the body of Christ. We have leadership such as pastors, worship leaders, psalmists, and ministry leaders forsaking their relationship with God for a greater ministry, greater financial gain, a greater reputation and notoriety. In essence, many leaders in the body of Christ have taken on the spirit of ahab and left worshipping the God of their salvation and have gone after other gods. They have been seduced by principalities and powers and have married religion, greed, the traditions of men, and all forms of false doctrines. There are even ministries which are teaching wives how to use sex to gain or maintain control over their husbands. And because the leadership is involved in this sort of abomination, their congregations are seduced, controlled and influenced by these same spirits. And by this act many of God's people are being offered up as sacrifices and perishing spiritually, relationally, financially, and in some ways even physically.

And it shall be, if thou do at all forget the LORD thy God, and walk after other gods, and serve them, and worship them, I testify against you this day that ye shall surely perish
Deuteronomy 8:19

Today many parts of the Church throughout the world are controlled and influenced by these same principalities.

There's an old saying which says, **"If you don't learn from your mistakes you're bound to repeat them."** *This can't be more accurate concerning the Church. We have not learned from the mistakes of those that have come before us. Rather than carefully studying and learning from the mistakes of the children of Israel, we have perpetuated those same mistakes thousands of years later. We tend to read the Old Testament as some fictional story line when in fact these were actual historical events. And it was for this reason that God recorded their errors so we would avoid repeating what they did and experiencing what God did.*

Now these things were our examples, to the intent we should not lust after evil things, as they also lusted. Neither be ye idolaters, as were some of them; as it is written, The people sat down to eat and drink, and rose up to play. Neither let us commit fornication, as some of them committed, and fell in one day three and twenty thousand. Neither let us tempt Christ, as some of them also tempted, and were destroyed of serpents. Neither murmur ye, as some of them also murmured, and were destroyed of the destroyer. Now all these things happened unto them for examples: and they are written for our admonition, upon whom the ends of the world are come. Wherefore let him that thinketh he standeth take heed lest he fall
I Corinthians 10:5-12

Building their own kingdoms

*A simple definition for the word kingdom is, **"the king's way of doing things."** It is the system of the will, ways, and laws of the king or monarch established and operating in the hearts of willing and obedient citizens or subjects. That being said, I want to share with you a word that was shared with a group of pastors, prophets, and intercessors during a time of worship and intercession.*

Every 2nd Friday of the month musicians, psalmists, pastors, intercessors, and prophets come together in our city for what we call "harp and bowl sessions." This is a time of worship, prayer, and prophecy. As the music is playing men and women in the congregation would receive a word of knowledge, a prophecy, or a burden from the heart of God to lift it up to Him in prayer.

During one of these sessions, a Sudanese pastor came up to the mike and began to share with us what the Lord revealed to him concerning our city. He shared with us that when he came to our town, he sensed something wasn't right in the city. He was very uneasy and began to pray and ask God what was going on in this city. The Lord revealed to him 3 things; One, there was a dragon over this city influencing many people. Two, many of the people that were being influenced in the city were pastors. And three, the Lord told him that many pastors in this city have forsaken the kingdom of God and are building their own kingdoms. They were more concerned about building their own legacy than fulfilling the will of God and teaching others in their ministry and congregation to do their will rather than the will of God.

In essence the system of God's way of doing things has been replaced with the pastor's or leadership's way of doing things and ultimately the enemy's way of doing things. Like ahab, they have forsaken the will and ways of the Almighty, becoming insensitive to the leadings, unctions, and warnings of God-the Holy Spirit, and have opened themselves, their families, their leadership and congregation up to an unholy system of government and all forms of fleshly and demonic influence, false teachings, lust, lies and seduction.

**Now the Spirit speaketh expressly, that in the latter times some shall depart from the faith, giving heed to seducing spirits, and doctrines of devils; Speaking lies in hypocrisy; having their conscience seared with a hot iron
I Timothy 4:1,2**

Like in the days of ahab, this dark system of the enemy, working through the hard hearted and carnal mind, has taken hold of many parts of the body of Christ in our day. It has replaced the move of the Holy Spirit, along with His standards, statutes and ordinances with the traditions of men, religious rituals, and seductive, deception tactics of the enemy. It possesses a form of godliness (the operation of deception), it's operating in its ordinances and standards (the operation of religious spirits), but it denies (the operation of the spirit of rebellion) the power of God. God wants to save, heal, deliver, and use His people. But the move of the Holy Spirit in many areas of the body has been replaced with the operation of the flesh and the seductive tactics of satan.

45

The restoration of the government of God

And it came to pass after many days, that the word of the LORD came to Elijah in the third year, saying, Go, show thyself unto Ahab…And Elijah went to show himself unto Ahab
I Kings 18:1,2

I believe the greatest conflict in the history of Christianity is about to break forth in the Church. The conflict we see in the earth today will pale in comparison to what's about to take place. This conflict will not only affect the body of Christ, but all of society, and even all of creation.

As Israel and their wicked government were going about their daily affairs without God, there was another order, a divine government, waiting in the wings in anticipation for the moment when God will say, **"God, show thyself unto ahab."**

This holy order has been in a long season of obscurity and development by the Holy Spirit, being prepared for the day of confrontation and restoration of all that is holy and righteous. And just as the prophet of God appeared without warning or thunderous fan fair (I Kings 17:1), this new apostolic prophetic order will come forth in unbridled passion, power, and authority to speak to the established corrupted and idolatrous order that God is the King of glory.

In I Kings 18:1,2, we see the Lord coming to Elijah, informing him that the time has come for Him (God) to be glorified in the sight of all Israel and the world.

46

It is time for the glory of God to confront the wicked system that has been in place in the body of Christ for hundreds of years. It's time to confront the principalities and powers that have deceived and seduced the people of God and the world that their hour of control and dominance is at an end.

As Elijah meets ahab in I Kings 18:17, we hear the king say to Elijah, "art thou he that troubleth Israel?" This statement reveals the depths of the kings dark deceived heart and the control the enemy has over his thinking and perspective. We see in this statement that he and all of Israel have been so influenced by the powers of darkness that they consider good evil and evil good.

> **Woe unto them that call evil good, and good evil; that put darkness for light, and light for darkness; that put bitter for sweet, and sweet for bitter**
> **Isaiah 5:20**

This is prevalent throughout the body of Christ. We see so many things that have been taught and performed for so long in the Church it's construed as being divine when the truth is it's carnally motivated and demonically influenced.

We've heard men and women of God bring a true word from the Lord countless times correcting us in our way of doing things. And countless times they have been rejected because it speaks against the established system of government. They reject the word of God not realizing they have not only rejected the messenger and the message, they have also rejected God (I Samuel 8:4-7; Luke 10:16).

47

As ahab stood before Elijah accusing him of being the guilty party of all of Israel's troubles, Elijah stands in divine defiance against the idolatrous king and proclaims to him:

> **I have not troubled Israel; but thou, and thy father's house, in that ye have forsaken the commandments of the LORD, and thou hast followed Baalim**
> **I Kings 18:18**

Elijah represents a people coming forth in the land, walking in the power, boldness, and authority of the kingdom of God. These are people who will not only declare the gospel, but they will also walk in the demonstration of the Spirit. Nations will turn back to God, not because they heard the word only, but because they've seen the power of God.

> **And I, brethren, when I came to you, came not with excellency of speech or of wisdom, declaring unto you the testimony of God. For I determined not to know any thing among you, save Jesus Christ, and him crucified. And I was with you in weakness, and in fear, and in much trembling. And my speech and my preaching was not with enticing words of man's wisdom, but in demonstration of the Spirit and of power: That your faith should not stand in the wisdom of men, but in the power of God**
> **I Corinthians 2:1-5**

48

He represents a people subject and obedient to the Lord, walking in righteousness, opposing the unrighteousness of the world and the kingdom of darkness. He represents a people who have taken on the very character and nature of the Almighty.

We will see a remnant rising up in the body of Christ, walking in oneness with the Spirit of God, completely submitted to and controlled by the Spirit. These people will walk a complete holiness and intimacy with the Lord.

And I looked, and, lo, a Lamb stood on the mount Zion, and with him a hundred forty and four thousand, having his Father's name written in their foreheads. And I heard a voice from heaven, as the voice of many waters, and as the voice of a great thunder: and I heard the voice of harpers harping with their harps: And they sung as it were a new song before the throne, and before the four beasts, and the elders: and no man could learn that song but the hundred and forty and four thousand, which were redeemed from the earth. These are they which were not defiled with women; for they are virgins. These are they which follow the Lamb whithersoever he goeth. These were redeemed from among men, being the firstfruits unto God and to the Lamb. And in their mouth was found no guile: for they are without fault before the throne of God Revelation 14:1-5

A showdown before the nations

***And he shall thrust out the enemy from before
thee; and shall say, Destroy them
Deuteronomy 33:27***

*As the event unfolds, we see the prophet of God
confronting the king and the entire nation of Israel
concerning their backslidden state and idolatrous ways. He
speaks to their hearts saying they have forsaken the God of
their fathers. They have forgotten who they were and have
given themselves over to the god of this world. And as a
result, this seductive malicious spirit has darkened the minds
of the entire nation and has caused them to compromise their
godly heritage and relationship with the One and only true
and living God.*

***But if our gospel be hid, it is hid to them that
are lost: In whom the god of this world hath
blinded the minds of them which believe not,
lest the light of the glorious gospel of Christ,
who is the image of God, should shine unto
them
II Corinthians 4:3,4***

*We find that this scripture applies, not only to those
who are not saved, but to many of us who are saved as well.*
*Then, the prophet Elijah challenges, not only Israel,
but the prophets of baal. He challenges Israel and those in
power to prove whether their god is the true god.*

I believe that the coming showdown will not be conducted in some small church over in some little rural part of the land. It won't be in a storefront church or at a prayer breakfast. But this showdown between the powers of darkness and the power of Almighty God will be seen on every television, in every stadium, before the governments of the world, and on every street in the land. This battle will be for all the marbles. This showdown will show once and for all who is the true God and billions will turn to the Lord in a day all over the world. Even now we see on the television in the marketplaces, the educational system, the entertainment systems, the justice systems and governmental systems of the world the enemy dancing before the nations of the world, demonstrating their power, seducing millions into believing that their way is the right way. But what we are seeing in this historic event we will also see transpire in our generation.

Even as the enemies of Lord Jesus came by night to capture Him (the night being symbolic of darkness and deception clouding the minds of the people), this was their hour to try and prove that their religious god was the true god. This is the hour we're in today, the power of darkness.

Then Jesus said unto the chief priests, and captains of the temple, and the elders, which were come to him, Be ye come out, as against a thief, with swords and staves? When I was daily with you in the temple, ye stretched forth no hands against me: but this is your hour, and the power of darkness
Luke 22:52,53

The Coming Civil War

We see this darkness moving throughout the body of Christ in many ways in many forms and fashions. We see the word of God being used in manipulative ways for financial gain. We see preachers around the world imparting fear into the hearts of congregations in order to maintain membership in their system of government. We see many singers, rather than ministering to the Lord through their gift of song, they entertain the people for project sales, royalties and notoriety.

We see many people striving for positions of authority, respect, and control by obtaining titles such as bishop, doctor, etc. We hear preaching going forth about prosperity when in fact it's really preaching on greed.

Now let me qualify these remarks. This activity isn't happening everywhere in the Church. There are people who haven't bowed the knee, but have given themselves wholly to the Lord to serve Him and Him alone. These are they whom God will raise up and demonstrate His power and authority.

Let us keep in mind God isn't necessarily doing this as a form of judgment, but for His love toward His people.

Turn, O backsliding children, saith the LORD;
for I am married unto you: and I will take you
one of a city, and two of a family, and I will
bring you to Zion
Jeremiah 3:14

He's doing this to keep His promise to His servant David (Isaiah 37:35). He's doing this to keep His covenant to the patriarchs Abraham, Isaac, and Jacob (II Kings 13:23). He's doing this for Himself and for His glory (Isaiah 43:5-7).

He's doing this in order for His kingdom to come and for His will to be done in the earth as it is in the heavens.

At the hour of the evening sacrifice the prophet of God calls all of Israel to attention. The hour is coming where the word of the Lord will go forth throughout the land and all will hear the sound of the Lord's call. They will hear and see the glory of God upon His Apostolic and prophetic people and they will come to attention to hear what the Spirit has to say, not only to the Church, but to all the world.

And the LORD shall be seen over them, and his arrow shall go forth as the lightning: and the Lord GOD shall blow the trumpet Zechariah 9:14

As they fix their eyes on the man of God he begins to rebuild the altar of the Lord. He doesn't use the altar of the prophets of baal use, for their altar is founded on darkness, deception, and demonic control. For there is no other foundation the prophet of God stands and builds upon but that foundation which the Lord of Glory has established.

For other foundation can no man lay than that is laid, which is Jesus Christ I Corinthians 3:11

The prophet uses twelve stones unaltered by human hands or instruments (Exodus 20:25). This symbolizes the restoring of the government of God not made with human hands and restoring the altar of God and prayer in the earth.

All around the world we see spirit of prayer and intercession moving throughout the land being reestablished in the hearts of God's people as the focal point and foundation for the government and the glory of God to be released in the earth. Men and women along with young people are filling stadiums around the nations crying out to God to hear our prayers, forgive us of our sins and heal the land with a mighty revival.

After the man of God prepares the evening sacrifice he does something very interesting and prophetic. He tells those around him to take four barrels of water and pour the water upon the sacrifice three times. This a prophetic picture of the outpouring of the Holy Spirit-kingdom of God-the government of God upon those of us who have presented themselves as living sacrifices unto the God of their salvation. This will be an awesome demonstration of the Spirit of the living God operating through those who have placed themselves upon the altar of God's government, giving themselves over to prayer and intercession, dying to self and yielding to the presence and power of almighty God. Many will walk in the fullness of God's character and nature, walking in the fullness of God's authority and power, declaring it is not I that lives but Christ that lives within me.

I am crucified with Christ: nevertheless I live; yet not I, but Christ liveth in me: and the life which I now live in the flesh I live by the faith of the Son of God, who loved me, and gave himself for me
Galatians 2:20

Then after all was set the prophet of God lifts his hands and heart to heaven and says:

LORD God of Abraham, Isaac, and of Israel, let it be known this day that thou art God in Israel, and that I am thy servant, and that I have done all these things at thy word. Hear me, O LORD, hear me, that this people may know that thou art the LORD God, and that thou hast turned their heart back Again
I Kings 18:36,37

And before the man of God could scarcely finish his prayers God sends a mighty answer. Look what happens:

Then the fire of the LORD fell, and consumed the burnt sacrifice, and the wood, and the stones, and the dust, and licked up the water that was in the trench. And when all the people saw it, they fell on their faces: and they said, The LORD, he is the God; the LORD, he is the God
I Kings 18:38,39

This one powerful demonstration by God turned an entire nation back to God in one moment, in one day. In this one power encounter the entire idolatrous, demonic structure was totally brought down and destroyed. When the people saw this it lifted the dark cloud that covered the minds of the people and open their eyes to the fact that God, He is God!

The Coming Civil War

People of God we are about the experience the greatest demonstration of the power of God that hasn't been seen since the day when God raised His son Jesus from the grave and exalted Him high above all principalities, powers, and rulers and has given Him a name above all names.

In the coming outpouring of God's fire we'll see millions both in the Church and around the world confess that Jesus is Lord to the glory of God the Father. We will see the entire demonic structure of satan come down in the governmental system, in the entertainment system, in the educational system, in the family structure, in the medical system, in the justice system, and the economical system and the government of God restored to its rightful place in the hearts of men, women, boys, and girls around the world. We will see unity and peace joy and praise restored to the Church. We will speak the same thing, preach the same thing and pray the same thing because we will be filled with and led by the same blessed Holy Spirit (Psalm 133).

Salvation, healing, deliverance, signs and wonders, and miracles will be a common occurrence around the world. Not only Churches will be filled but stadiums will be used to hold prayer gatherings and Sunday services everywhere. Crime will all but vanish in the streets. The prisons will become no different than the house of God because the Spirit of the Lord will fill prisons and men and women will be saved and used for the kingdom. Many that are imprisoned for crimes they didn't commit will be released and compensated for the injustice committed against them and their families.

When the fire of God's presence is released the world will never be the same again. To God be the glory!

56

Chapter 5
An Enemy is in the house

**And a man's foes shall be they of his own
household
Matthew 10:36**

I shared in the last chapter how God was using me and
my best friend who is now my pastor in the ministry of
intercession. As He was using us and others who were a part
of the intercessors ministry God was doing some powerful
things in our time of intercession and in the Sunday morning
services. Many were being blessed, healed, delivered, and
souls were being saved. And as a result of allowing God to
have His way the Church was growing in numbers, in
character, and moving forward in fulfilling its destiny.

The prophetic was flowing powerfully and we were
growing individually in sensitivity and intimacy in the Spirit.

But there were some in leadership and the
congregation who opposed what was happening and one of
those who opposed us and what God was doing was our chief
intercessor. The chief intercessor was being influenced not
just by their own traditional convictions concerning
intercession, but was also being influenced by leadership who
had a problem with what was happening because of jealousy,
envy, competition, control, and pride. They walked in an
attitude of condescension that implied that if God was going
to use anyone to do what was being done it should have been
them. And because God was using a bunch of "no names"
they took issue with it and began to speak against what was
happening. But the more they persecuted us, the more God
increased in us and the more He was glorified.

The Coming Civil War

Sadly, the outcome of this story was because of their position in the church and their influence over the chief intercessor and the senior pastor, the church's intercessory prayer ministry was shut down and minimized to just kneeling at the altar and sitting in the pew and praying, thus quenching and shutting down the move of the Holy Spirit.

There was a time when I couldn't believe that men and women who profess to be deeply in love with God would suddenly turn against God. It was difficult for me to comprehend such an act of treason. But in studying the word of God, reviewing past revivals, hearing what the Holy Spirit was saying, and hearing what others have personally experienced, it has brought me to this disheartening conclusion. Many of God's people will become an enemy in the coming move of God. I tried in many ways to blame satan's influence for those who would oppose what God is going to do. But God has revealed to me the enemy will be involved, but many will know what they're doing (Matthew 28:1-7,11-13).

As a result of this event and others, this ministry has been overrun by all forms of demonic activity. The pastor's heart has become hard towards the people of God. Many of the people of God have been deeply wounded and have backslidden, refusing to step back into a Church and some have even died. Many have become involved with immoral and corrupted activities, and even those who came against the intercessory prayer ministry when we were there have left that ministry because of the abuse they themselves have experienced. You might think this is well deserved. But I feel otherwise.

This ministry is a part of the kingdom of God that was called to do great things in the earth and glorify the King of kings and yet it has become a place of death and destruction. This is just a small example of what we can expect in the next move of the Holy Spirit, but on a global scale.

I cannot stress to you the importance of making prayer, along with the word of God our foundation in the Church and in our personal lives. Spirit-led prayer opens the heavens over our lives and those whom our prayers are targeting. Prayer releases the move of the Holy Spirit in our lives and ministry. Prayer exposes and destroys the works of darkness. Prayer births unity and peace. Prayer changes our perspective from carnal to spiritual. Prayer reveals the will of God and His strategy for its fulfillment. And prayer builds the character and nature of God, revealing Christ within us.

Prayer opens our eyes to see, not only what the enemy is doing (II Kings 6:8-12), but what the Father is doing also (John 5:19). Prayer can change the heart of God and bring restoration and peace (Isaiah 38:1-5).

A true prophetic voice and intercessor who gives themselves over to praying and declaring the will of God in the earth will transcend the boundaries of tradition, control, and religion and reach the endless expanse of eternity. A true prophetic intercessors has the potential to possess and demonstrate the power and authority of the Spirit to literally change the course of humanity and the nations of the world.

I love reading the quotes of men and women of God who were generals of prayer. Even though they have gone on to be with the Lord many years ago, their words on prayer still carry the anointing and power of God.

59

How long will it take us to learn that our shortest route to the man next door is by way of God's throne?
A.T. Pierson

I have learned by experience that it is not much labor but much prayer that is the only means to success
Andrew Bonar

The reason why many fail in battle is because they wait until the hour of battle. The reason why others succeed is because they have gained their victory on tier knees long before the battle came...Anticipate your battles; fight them on your knees before temptation comes, and you will always have victory
R.A. Torrey

I would rather train twenty men to pray, than a thousand to preach; A minister's highest mission ought to be to teach his people to pray
H. MacGregor

Prayer will make a man cease from sin, or sin will entice a man to cease from prayer. Pray often; for prayer is a shield to the soul, a sacrifice to God, and a scourge for satan
John Bunyan

**They who pray not, know nothing of God, nor
of the state of their souls
Adam Clarke**

**The great battles, the battles that decide our
destiny and the destiny of generations yet
unborn, are not fought on public platforms,
but in the lonely hours of the night and in
moments of agony
Samuel Logan Brengle**

As we study Matthew 10, Lord Jesus gave His disciples power to demonstrate the kingdom of God. He imparts to them a foretaste of the authority and power of the Holy Spirit through personal experience of what's to come in the days ahead through the demonstration of the Holy Spirit in their lives. And in obedience to the word of the Lord they go forth throughout the land preaching the gospel of the kingdom and releasing the power of God into the lives of the oppressed.

Excitement and hunger fills their hearts as they minister to the lost and broken children of Israel (Luke 4:18,19; Luke 10:17-19). He instructs them to heal the sick, raise the dead and cast out demons. He tells them where to go and what to do when they get there. But as He speaks with them He tells His disciples to demonstrate the power and preach the kingdom of God only in the house of Israel. And He goes on to share that it is within the house of Israel that they will experience great persecution and warfare. In other words it is among their own brethren that they will experience their greatest attacks.

**These twelve Jesus sent forth, and commanded
them, saying, Go not into the way of the
Gentiles, and into any city of the Samaritans
enter ye not: But go rather to the lost sheep of
the house of Israel...Behold, I send you forth
as sheep in the midst of wolves: be ye therefore
wise as serpents, and harmless as doves. But
beware of men: for they will deliver you up to
the councils, and they will scourge you in their
synagogues...And the brother shall deliver up
the brother to death, and the father the child:
and the children shall rise up against their
parents, and cause them to be put to death
Matthew 10:5,6,16,17,21**

*When the Holy Spirit is poured out there will be a
separation between those who are open and yielded to the
will and operation of the Lord and those who will choose to
remain in their religious and traditional forms of worship. In
the next move of the Holy Spirit the intents and motives of
men's hearts shall be revealed and will bring about a civil
war in families, relationships, and in the house of God.*

**Think not that I am come to send peace on
earth: I came not to send peace, but a sword.
For I am come to set a man at variance
against his father, and the daughter against
her mother, and the daughter-in- law against
her mother-in-law
Matthew 10:34,35**

When the move of God came to Israel in the form of Lord Jesus a division began to take place in the Land. Those who were open and hungry for more of God began to follow Lord Jesus and those that opposed the move of God remained devoted to the established religious order and began to persecute what God was doing through Lord Jesus.

There will be a people that will come out of the body of Christ that will move in the power and demonstration of the Spirit. This company of believers will not only move in the demonstration of the Spirit-healing, delivering, and saving souls, but they will move in the love, joy, and peace of the Spirit. By this divine manifestation through these believers they will draw many out of the darkness of religious ways and the traditions of men and introduce them to the same glorious experience they themselves have yielded to.

But there will be those who will extremely oppose this new experience. They will view what God is going to do as a threat and detriment to their established way of doing things, knowing that it is the Lord's doing. They will speak against the next move of the Holy Spirit, they will call those anointed men and women of God who are under the divine influence and control of the Holy Spirit trouble makers, deceivers, heretics, and even demon possessed. Many will come against the new move of the Spirit, persecuting the followers of Lord Jesus with verbal assaults, attempted character assignation, and will go to the point of physical persecution. They will put fear into the hearts of their followers by calling this company of believers a cult, devil worshipers, and fanatics to keep their following bound to their form of godliness while denying the power of the Almighty.

The War within the Kingdom

***Now there was long war between the house of
Saul and the house of David: but David waxed
stronger and stronger, and the house of Saul
waxed weaker and weaker
II Samuel 3:1***

The war between the house of Saul and the house of
David is a symbolic war in the Church between the flesh and
the Spirit. The house of Saul is the operation of the flesh
fighting to maintain its rule and way of doing things while the
house of David is a picture of the move of God rising in
Apostolic prophetic power, favor, praise, worship, and love.

The house of Saul is symbolic of the operation of the
works of the flesh, looking only to fulfill its lust of self
gratification, control, and dominion. The house of Saul are
those who only desire to do things their way, not willing to
walk in complete obedience to the will of God but will do
things their way, expecting God to conform to their ways.

The house of Saul, although they were ordained and
anointed by God, began walking in the ways of God, failed
God by deviating from the purposes and plans of God. The
house of Saul are those who refuse to change. Because of
their lust for power and control they will attack everyone who
rises up against their form of godliness because they view
them as a threat to their position of dominance.

The house of Saul represents those who oppress and
persecute the David's of the kingdom. They represent the
abusive, manipulating, controlling, javelin- throwing order.

Saul is symbolic of a rebellious religious system not willing to obey, refusing to change and desperately trying to hold on to tradition and their position of power, control and influence over a people.

Saul is also a picture of a body of dysfunctional religious leadership walking in insecurity, low self-esteem, competition, and a lack of identity of who they are in God.

Saul is a picture of a people anointed and chosen by God to do a work for the kingdom but through self exaltation became a god unto themselves, they became hard-hearted and insensitive, not only to the people of God, but to God Himself.

These are they that will attack anyone that comes against their way of operation. Rather than seeing those whom God uses as an asset to build and expansion of the kingdom of God they look at them as competitors and threats to their position and way of doing things even though they know it's God moving through them (I Samuel 18:10-12).

They see the favor of God on their lives. They see how much more they can do for the kingdom of God. They see how many souls their leading to new levels of God, not drawing them unto themselves but leading them to the King of kings.

They see how gifted they are. They see their intimate relationship with the Lord and how they are able to worship and praise God, creating an atmosphere conducive to healing, deliverance, revelation, and salvation. They see how they can ignite the hearts of the people to pursue God and God alone. They even see how effective they are in defeating the enemy and setting the captives free. Even though this Davidic company will love and be devoted to the house of Saul, Saul will still view them as a danger to their kingdom.

And just as Saul eyed David through the eyes of control, jealousy, envy, and insecurity, they will eye the Davidic people of God, looking for a way to kill them in character, and spirituality, and as the enemy increases its influence, they may even attempt to literally kill them (Acts 7).

But the house of David is otherwise minded. They are a people of love, humility, and passion for the presence of God. They're not concerned with position, title, fortune, fame and notoriety. Their only concern is that Lord Jesus is exalted and the kingdom and the glory of God covers the earth as the waters cover the sea. They have a heart for souls. They walk in the realm of the Spirit and aggressively oppose the things of the flesh and the enemy.

They're not intimidated by the gifts of others for they know those gifts are for the Lord's pleasure and they will be used for the glory of God. And when they see the grace of God on the lives of other men and women of God they will not be jealous, intimidated, envious, or threatened, but they will rejoice and encourage them to continue to contend for the faith and fulfill the will of God with unbridled passion, not compromising their place in God and defending it without apology or respect of person.

The house of David is passionate and hungry for the presence of God. They possess a hunger and a thirst for the presence God that cannot be quenched nor satisfied. Their passion is not in earthly things. They're not interested in being seen and acknowledge by man. They could care less if their name is known. Their pursuits are not for fortune. But their desire is to please God. They're focus is on meeting the needs of the King and fulfilling His heart's desires.

66

Even while they're performing their daily affairs their minds and hearts are consumed with being alone with the Lord of glory in intimate communion, praise, worship, and prayer.

As this long war between the house of Saul and the house David continues, we will see a gradual shift of the established order within the Church. We will see the religious and man-made traditional order of Saul, void of the presence and power of God begin to weaken. Their membership and resources will begin to dwindle. Relationships and people they once relied on will begin to strangely disappear. They will unfortunately become a shadow of their former selves, once living to glorify God, but now living only for themselves and their religious way of doing things. And eventually these ministries will shut down and they will no longer exist.

Cain and Abel

And Cain talked with Abel his brother: and it came to pass, when they were in the field, that Cain rose up against Abel his brother, and slew him
Genesis 4:8

Cain and Abel were the sons of Adam. Cain was a tiller of the ground, a farmer if you will, and Abel was a shepherd. Both knew the voice of God and heard from the Lord to bring Him an offering. So Cain brought forth an offering which was from the ground and Abel brought forth the firstlings of his flock. God approved of Abel's offering but He rejected Cain's offering.

The Coming Civil War

Both heard the same word from the Lord concerning what type of offering to present to Him. But both responded in different manners.

You might say, when did God speak with Cain and Abel to bring forth an offering. Well, Lets Look at Hebrews:

By faith Abel offered unto God a more excellent sacrifice than Cain, by which he obtained witness that he was righteous
Hebrews 11:4

Abel opened his heart to the word of the Lord and was obedient to His will by offering up to God an excellent sacrifice that transcended that of Cain's. Abel was declared righteous because of his faith in God's word.

So then faith cometh by hearing, and hearing by the word of God
Romans 10:17

As a result of Abel's obedience to God's word by offering an acceptable sacrifice to God, God blessed Abel and he received favor from the Lord.

Now Cain heard the same word from the Lord. He had the same opportunity to receive the blessing and favor of the Lord because God is no respecter of persons (Acts 10:34). But because of self-righteousness, pride, arrogance, and control, he chose to deviate from the plan of God and present to God that which was cursed (Genesis 3:17), thereby, God rejecting his offering. And this is where the war begins.

68

Because of God's rejection of his offering, Cain became so enraged and jealous over Abel's relationship with God that Cain rose up and killed his own brother.

Cain is symbolic of a people in the Church filled with self-righteousness, pride, arrogance, and control that walk in their own way of doing things, expecting God to sanction what they produce rather than doing what God commands. They walk in a spirit of entitlement, rebellion, and personal idolatry, thinking they deserve what God has for them regardless of their actions, knowing that anything they produce in their own flesh is cursed and will be rejected by the Almighty. But because of pride and self-righteousness, rather than repenting for their rebellion, they will rise up and attack those who are the obedient of God.

And as it was in the days of Cain and Abel it will be in the coming move of God. As the obedient of God go forth in the righteousness and favor of the Lord, doing the will of God in faith, offering up the sacrifices of praise, worshipping in the beauty of holiness and establishing the kingdom of God in love, power, and the demonstration of the Holy Spirit, we are going to see the religious, self-righteous, prideful, arrogant, and controlling body coming against the humble, meek, and obedient of the Lord, and taking steps through deception and a murdering spirit to do away with the righteous of God. But just as the spirit of Cain and Saul rise up against the people of God, God will reveal the plans of the enemy, shut down the attacks of satan and make a way of escape for His people.

God shall reveal even this unto you
Philippians 3:15

The Coming Civil War

We are in a paradigm that demands deep intimate relationship with the Holy Spirit. There is no other relationship more vital in this day and time as our relationship with God-the Holy Spirit. Unless we give ourselves fully to the will, work, and communion of the Lord we will find ourselves being drawn away like our brethren in our own lust and seduced by the subtle tactics of the enemy.

Love is what's going to win lost souls to the Lord. As we look at the body of Christ we see this term "lost souls" isn't just relegated to those who are unsaved but also to those who are saved. It is spiritual paradox to say there are many in Christ that are still lost, but it is very, very true.

*But the Holy Spirit just revealed to me" **there is a difference between those who have Christ in their hearts and those who are in Christ." ** There are many who are professing Christ as Savior, but few who profess Him as Savior AND Lord. Those submitting to Christ as Savior grants them a place in the kingdom, but those submitting to Christ as Lord sets them on the throne with Christ.*

It will be the responsibility of all of us who have submitted to the Lordship of Christ to reveal Christ in all of His fullness to those who have settled for the religious and traditional status quo. Only through the demonstration of the Holy Spirit can lost souls (saved and unsaved) come into the knowledge of the Truth and receive all that God has for them.

As I stated earlier, it's going to take the unconditional love of God to draw God's children into their ordained place in the kingdom. You and I have this great joy privilege and responsibility to submit to God and let Him use us to bring His people out of darkness and into His marvelous light.

70

Chapter 6
When kingdoms fall

And in the days of these kings shall the God of heaven set up a kingdom, which shall never be destroyed: and the kingdom shall not be left to other people, but it shall break in pieces and consume all these kingdoms, and it shall stand forever
Daniel 2:44

I shared with you earlier a story of a group of pastors, prophets, and intercessors coming together for a time of prayer for our city. During that time of prayer a Sudanese pastor came forth and shared with us what God revealed to him about the spiritual leadership and condition of our city. He stated that when he came to the city he felt uneasy in his spirit. He didn't know what it was, except that there was something not right about this city God called him to.

*He sought the Lord to find out what was this unrest in his spirit. He stated that the Lord said to him, **"many pastors in this city have left building my kingdom to build their own kingdom."** This brought deep conviction upon those of us who heard this disheartening revelation as we received witness from the Holy Spirit that this word was from the Lord.*

After hearing this word we immediately began to pray for God's forgiveness. Pastors in the gathering stood proxy for the shepherds of the city, asking for God forgiveness and to do a work in the hearts of the leadership in the city.

We're in a season of a great falling away. This falling away isn't so much as people literally leaving the Church as it is a falling away within the kingdom of God.

There is an internal apostasy taking place in the Church of the Living God. Men and women of God are deviating from the flow of the Spirit and moving in their flesh and being seduced by the enemy thus moving contrary to the purposes and plans of the Almighty, becoming a god unto themselves or unfortunately becoming instruments of darkness, being used by the enemy.

Now the Spirit speaketh expressly, that in the latter times some shall depart from the faith, giving heed to seducing spirits, and doctrines of devils; Speaking lies in hypocrisy; having their conscience seared with a hot iron
I Timothy 4:1,2

There is so much that can be said concerning the spiritual condition of the Church. As a body we've become what we were supposed to have been delivered from-a church filled with the ways and desires of the world. We've become so consumed with the lust for power, money, position, notoriety, and the need to be entertained, we've become totally insensitive to the cry of God-the Holy Spirit that says:

For I am the LORD that bringeth you up out of the land of Egypt, to be your God: ye shall therefore be holy, for I amHoly...Wherefore come out from among them, and be ye separate, saith the Lord, and touch not the unclean thing; and I will receive you
Leviticus 11:45; II Corinthians 6:17

When kingdoms fall

And in the days of these kings shall the God of heaven set up a kingdom which shall never be destroyed. *The kingdom of God in its most basic definition is "God's way of doing things established and operating in the lives of His people." It is the character and nature of Lord Jesus manifesting by the Holy Spirit through those who have given themselves over to the presence, power, and will of God.*

For I will take you from among the nations and gather you out of all countries and bring you into your own land. Then will I sprinkle clean water upon you, and you shall be clean from all your uncleanness; and from all your idols will I cleanse you. A new heart will I give you and a new spirit will I put within you, and I will take away the stony heart out of your flesh and give you a heart of flesh. And I will put my Spirit within you and cause you to walk in My statutes, and you shall heed My ordinances and do them. And you shall dwell in the land that I gave to your fathers; and you shall be My people, and I will be your God
Ezekiel 36:24-28
The Amplified Version

Although this speaks of Passover and Pentecost, we are about the see a move of the Spirit that transform the yielded men and women of God within the body of Christ.

73

The Coming Civil War

The next outpouring of the Holy Spirit will not just dwell within men's hearts, but He will literally possess the souls of those who submit to His will. This manifestation will release a massive outpouring of healing and deliverance, miracles, signs and wonders and through these powerful demonstrations we'll see the greatest harvest of souls the world and the Church has every seen in history.

In this powerful release of the Spirit we'll see the full character of Christ manifesting in the lives of His chosen people. This manifestation will also release an major and rapid increase of maturity in the body of Christ to prepare us for the literal return of our bridegroom, Lord Jesus.

For this cause I bow my knees unto the Father of our Lord Jesus Christ, Of whom the whole family in heaven and earth is named, That he would grant you, according to the riches of his glory, to be strengthened with might by his Spirit in the inner man; That Christ may dwell in your hearts by faith; that ye, being rooted and grounded in love, May be able to comprehend with all saints what is the breadth, and length, and depth, and height; And to know the love of Christ, which passeth knowledge, that ye might be filled with all the fullness of God
Ephesians 3:14-19

In this next great move of God we will see entire cities and nations come to Christ.

When God begins to retake His purchased possession through this move of the Spirit, this demonstration of the Lordship of King Jesus will be the beginning of the end of all kingdoms that have been set up both in the world and in the Church, thus producing a war between flesh, religion, traditions of men and the enemy verses the righteousness, peace, joy, and power of God and His kingdom people.

Now there was long war between the house of Saul and the house of David: but David waxed stronger and stronger, and the house of Saul waxed weaker and weaker
II Samuel 3:1

A modern day war between the house of David and the house of Saul is inevitable. It is a time when God invades the religious and demonic norm established in men's hearts and brings about a major disruption by rearranging the way things have been done causing a carnal backlash against the spiritual activity of God. I encourage you to study the history of past revivals of the Spirit. During your study you'll find there has never been a move of God that has never been attacked by His own people. But as the move of God continued you'll see one aspect of the Church grow in numbers and power but you'll see another aspect of the Church diminish in power and numbers and slowly but surely slip into obscurity. Those who have great influence in the body who spoke against what God was doing were eventually discredited and lost that influence and power by the fruit of what they were opposing or met with unfortunate incidents.

75

This will be evident again in the next move of the Holy Spirit.

We'll see those operating in a Saul mentality coming against those operating in a David mentality because of insecurity, control, and competition. But the key to the Davidic company becoming stronger and stronger and the Saul company becoming weaker and weaker will be contrast between the obedience, love and selflessness David walks in and the disobedience, pride, jealousy, and selfishness Saul walks in.

This demonstration of love from David will draw many from the house of Saul to the house David. Many will see the love, joy, peace, and prosperity the Davidic company will experience and will come out of the bondage of Saul. Some will come out not concerned with the persecution that will come with their departure from the control of Saul. And there will be some who will come out secretly for fear of what people will say or do to them like Nicademus who for fear of what his peers may say came to Jesus by night (John 3:1,2).

And the kingdom shall not be left to other people

I am the LORD: that is my name: and my glory will I not give to another, neither my praise to graven images
Isaiah 42:8

This next move of God will not be a move where men and women will be the focal point. But it will be a move that will put Lord Jesus at the center all that will be done in the body of Christ and in the lives of people around the world.

When God begins to move in the earth there will be awesome revelation of the fear and sovereignty of the Lord that will blanket the land. Owen Murphy, author of "When God stepped down from heaven," described revival as:

When men in the streets are afraid to open their mouths and utter godless words lest the judgments of God should fall; when sinners, overawed by the Presence of God tremble in the streets and cry for mercy; when, without special meetings and sensational advertising, the Holy Ghost sweeps across cities and towns in supernatural power and holds men in the grip of terrifying conviction; when every shop becomes a pulpit; every heart an altar; every home a sanctuary and people walk softly before God, this is revival!

The awesomeness of God's divine presence will grip the hearts of men and women around the world, leaving us in such a state of reverential fear and awe of God's presence we will not take a step to the left or right say anything without God's sanction.

Those who will try to take advantage of what God is going to do by seeking to place themselves in the limelight in order to make a name for themselves will find themselves being humbled by the Lord of glory. Only those clothed with humility and contrition, seeking not to do their will but the will of Him that sent them, will walk and dwell in the presence and glory of God.

77

The Coming Civil War

These men and women in all they say and do will put Christ at the center. They will walk in a divine obsession and passion for the presence of God. They will be the ones whom God will use to revive the hearts of the broken and bring light and life blessings to those who dwell in darkness and despair.

For thus saith the high and lofty One that inhabiteth eternity, whose name is Holy; I dwell in the high and holy place, with him also that is of a contrite and humble spirit, to revive the spirit of the humble, and to revive the heart of the contrite ones
Isaiah 57:15

But it shall break in pieces and consume all these kingdoms

Why do the heathen rage, and the people imagine a vain thing? The kings of the earth set themselves, and the rulers take counsel together, against the LORD, and against his anointed, saying, Let us break their bands asunder, and cast away their cords from us. He that sitteth in the heavens shall laugh: the Lord shall have them in derision. Then shall he speak unto them in his wrath, and vex them in his sore displeasure. Thou shalt break them with a rod of iron; thou shalt dash them in pieces like a potter's vessel
Psalm 2:1-5,9

The coming move of the kingdom of God isn't coming just to bless, heal, deliver, and save souls, but the move of God's kingdom is coming to destroy all that opposes His position as King of kings and dominion over the earth, both in and outside the Church. And He will do it through the chosen vessels prepared and fit for the Master's use. And through those same hands He has taught to war victoriously He will use to plant and build the kingdom of God around the world.

See, I have this day set thee over the nations and over the kingdoms, to root out, and to pull down, and to destroy, and to throw down, to build, and to plant
Jeremiah 1:10

And as God's army destroys all that man and the enemy has established, they will build according to the pattern of God's divine will (Exodus 25:40; Hebrews 8:5). Then King Jesus' prayer to the Father will be fulfilled.

Thy kingdom come. Thy will be done in earth, as it is in heaven
Matthew 6:10

And it shall stand forever

Thy kingdom is an everlasting kingdom, and thy dominion endureth throughout all generations
Psalm 145:13

T. Carlyle quoted, **"He who has no vision of eternity will never get a true hold of time."** *God's kingdom is an eternal kingdom. It is a kingdom that transcends time and space. It is a kingdom ruled by one King, the Lord Jesus Christ, King of kings and Lord of lords. When all other kingdoms have passed away, His kingdom will last for ever.*

While many are looking to build a temporary kingdom of self-exaltation, greed, lust, and power on this earthly plain, God has established a kingdom that will last far beyond anything man or satan can ever conceive or build. And God has raised up a people who are not looking to make the things of this world their kingdom but they're looking for an eternal kingdom where they've been called by their heavenly Father to rule and reign as kings and priest along side their Lord and Savior.

> **While we look not at the things which are seen, but at the things which are not seen: for the things which are seen are temporal; but the things which are not seen are eternal**
> **II Corinthians 4:18**

To understand what it means to be in an eternal kingdom we must understand eternal things. Like T. Carlyle stated, if you and I cannot come into the knowledge and perspective of eternal matters we will never put things in their proper place in our lives. And we will never realize the importance of our commission. We were not saved just to avoid eternal damnation, we were saved to fulfill the call of God for which we have been created and sent to this earth.

As we come into alignment with the eternal reality of God's kingdom we will change from a temporal perspective to an eternal one. In doing so we'll function from an eternal understanding and strive to accomplish eternal things.

Thy kingdom is an everlasting kingdom, and thy dominion endureth throughout all generations
Psalm 145:13

The kingdom of God is an enduring kingdom. It is a kingdom that has and will continue to endure the test of time. People have come and gone. Movements have come and gone. Future has become history and yet the kingdom of God was is and will always be the one thing that will never pass away. For thousands of years satan and carnal man have tirelessly attempted to destroy the kingdom of God. They've attempted to discredit the kingdom. They've attempted to outlaw the kingdom. They've even attempted to try and control the kingdom. But in the end the kingdom has endured the greatest onslaughts of man and satan. And as we approach the greatest manifestation of the kingdom the world has ever seen we'll literally see the transformation of all of society. Everything that doesn't line up with the eternal laws and standards of the kingdom of God will be done away. We will see changes on all levels of government. We will see changes in our educational system. We see changes in the social order. We'll see changes in the marketplace. And we will see the kingdom of God literally destroy every type of false religious practice in our world today.

The Coming Civil War

And in this next move of the Holy Spirit we'll see all kingdoms, nations, tribes, and tongues from all around the world both small and great, natural and spiritual flow to and come subject to the sovereign authority of our Lord and Savior, Jesus Christ.

And it shall come to pass in the end of days, that the mountain of Jehovah's house shall be established on the top of the mountains, and shall be lifted up above the hills; and all the nations shall flow unto it
Isaiah 2:2

Chapter 7
He must increase

He must increase, but I must decrease
John 3:30

It has not only been a privilege, an honor, and a blessing to be chosen and used by the Lord to write this book, but it has also been a challenge as well. To fulfill the will of the Lord in completing this work required me to die on a daily basis in order for the Holy Spirit to express Himself on the pages of this book. Along with the dying of my flesh, there were many spiritual attacks I encountered by the enemy, thus causing delays. There were even times during my meditating over this book that I even questioned whether or not this was the will of God or just an idea conjured up by my reasoning. But as I pressed on I began to realize there was a need that existed in the body of Christ. That need was the people of God needed to know not only what God was preparing to do, but what we need to do in preparing for what He was about to do. Along with this, the people of God must come to understand that we cannot afford to continue to perpetuate the mistakes of our spiritual forefathers that, because of a lack of biblical understanding, spiritual revelation and fear, they came against the very God they proclaimed to love. Some over a period of time, as they watched the fruit that was produced in the various outpourings of the Holy Spirit concluded this was truly of God. But there were some who knew what was taking place was of a divine origin and yet continued to refute, criticize and attack the move of God. This is why God has to take His people through seasons of deep workings to die to the will of the flesh, man's traditions and satan's influence.

83

If the increase of God's kingdom is going to be accomplished in the earth it isn't going to be done through the workings of man's hands, nor the eloquence of his speech, but it will only be completed through the inward submission of men's hearts to the glorious presence of God that lies within each believer.

But we have this treasure in earthen vessels, that the excellency of the power may be of God, and not of us...Always bearing about in the body the dying of the Lord Jesus, that the life also of Jesus might be made manifest in our body
II Corinthians 4:7,10

He must increase, but I must decrease
John 3:30

The key to the presence of God increasing in the earth lies in the submission of the people of God. God has the plan on how this will be accomplished but He needs you and I to come into agreement with His divine plan. And the only part God requires of us in His plan is submission and obedience.

*The word in John 3:30 that speaks the loudest to me is the word "must." This word says to me there are no other options to the plan of God in His presence increasing in the earth. HE **MUST** INCREASE. But the end of the passage is no less important, I **MUST** DECREASE. The first part is the responsibility of God the second part is the responsibility of the believer. We must decrease in order for Him to increase. In other words we must deny ourselves and submit to Him.*

84

The dying of self is the principle key to the increase of God's glory. There will never be a true revelation of the word, life and power of God without a dying of self through those whom He has chosen to fulfill this mandate in the earth.

Dying to self is evidence of a submissive and an obedient heart. No man or woman can be an instrument of God's increase in the earth without them coming into the mindset of obedience and submission to the will of God. And it is by you and me presenting ourselves as living sacrifices to God for the work of God's plan to be revealed and for increase to be implemented in our lives and in the earth.

I beseech you therefore, brethren, by the mercies of God, that ye present your bodies a living sacrifice, holy, acceptable unto God, which is your reasonable service. And be not conformed to this world: but be ye transformed by the renewing of your mind, that ye may prove what is that good, and acceptable, and perfect, will of God
Romans 12:1,2

The sacrificial presentation of the believer thus releasing the demonstration of the Spirit is the outward evidence of an inner working of the Lord in the lives of His people that have made the conscious decision that they have come into agreement with the will and plan of God. And as we continue to submit to the increase of God's presence in us and allow Him to demonstrate His love and power through us the world will see Him in us and acknowledge Jesus as Lord.

Of the increase of his government and peace
there shall be no end
Isaiah 9:7

The increase of the government of God depends upon the increase of the government of God within His people.

For I will take you from among the heathen,
and gather you out of all countries, and will
bring you into your own land. Then will I
sprinkle clean water upon you, and ye shall be
clean: from all your filthiness, and from all
your idols, will I cleanse you. A new heart also
will I give you, and a new spirit will I put
within you: and I will take away the stony
heart out of your flesh, and I will give you a
heart of flesh. And I will put my spirit within
you, and cause you to walk in my statutes, and
ye shall keep my judgments, and do them. And
ye shall dwell in the land that I gave to your
fathers; and ye shall be my people, and I will
be your God
Ezekiel 36:24-28

This is a quality issue not a quantity issue. Just as it is in the natural so it is in the spirit. When standards and laws of a government are corrupted, manipulated and distorted we produce a corrupted, manipulated and distorted people, walking in a double mindedness that knows not or in many ways resist the truth, resulting in a people unable to stand.

When the quality of God's government is established and increases in the hearts and minds of the people and demonstrated by inward operation of the Holy Spirit then we'll see an increase in the population of the government of God because their faith in and adherence to the standards are not in man's fleshly interpretations of God's laws nor in the deceitful workings of the enemy but by the experiential knowledge of their King, Lord and Savior.

And I, brethren, when I came to you, came not with excellency of speech or of wisdom, declaring unto you the testimony of God. For I determined not to know any thing among you, save Jesus Christ, and him crucified. And I was with you in weakness, and in fear, and in much trembling. And my speech and my preaching was not with enticing words of man's wisdom, but in demonstration of the Spirit and of power: That your faith should not stand in the wisdom of men, but in the power of God
I Corinthians 2:1-5

He must increase, but I must decrease
John 3:30

For one to decrease requires a humble heart a contrite spirit and a revelation of the utter filthiness of our carnal ways lying with each of us. But God must reveal it in order for cleansing humility and contrition to take place.

87

> **In the year that king Uzziah died I saw also
> the Lord sitting upon a throne, high and lifted
> up, and his train filled the temple...Then said
> I, Woe is me! for I am undone; because I am a
> man of unclean lips, and I dwell in the midst
> of a people of unclean lips: for mine eyes have
> seen the King, the LORD of hosts**
> **Isaiah 6:1,5**

The prophet Isaiah was the one who made the prophetic statement that the government and peace of God would increase. But that prophetic revelation could not have been revealed without Isaiah first seeing the King of kings, which revealed the ugliness of self, and producing a humble heart and contrite spirit (Isaiah 57:15). Through this experience God increased in power and revelation within the prophet to use Him to speak to Israel to return back to God.

You and I must receive a revelation of the King of glory. This is the need of the body of Christ. We need to see Lord Jesus not as the Lamb but as the sovereign King of the universe. And this will be the reality of many in the next move of God. We will see Him in a way we've never seen Him before. We will see Jesus as the King of kings in all of His glory, power, authority, and majesty.

Many will come into this sovereign and glorious reality of the holiness and majesty of Lord Jesus which will produce such a revelation of our uncleanness that it will bring us into complete humility of heart and contrition of spirit. By this divine experience we will see an uprising of God's people the world has never seen before in the history of the Church.

We will see a people filled with the power of God walking in the character of the Son fulfilling the will of the Spirit walking in the reverential fear of the Lord and the overwhelming gratitude of a soul that has a revelation of one who has been plucked from the fires of hell through the saving grace of the Father through Lord Jesus.

Through this we'll see the increase and peace of God's government both in quality and in quantity in the lives of His people will take His glory to the nations and cover the earth as the waters cover the sea saving souls destroying the works of darkness and preparing the way for coming of our King and our God, Jesus.